# 12 INCREDIBLE FACTS ABOUT THE
# CUBAN MISSILE CRISIS

by Sue Bradford Edwards

12 STORY
LIBRARY

www.12StoryLibrary.com

12-Story Library is an imprint of Peterson Publishing Company and Press Room Editions.

Produced for 12-Story Library by Red Line Editorial

Photographs ©: Corbis, cover, 1, 23; Deutsche Fotothek/Picture-Alliance/DPA/AP Images, 4; Berliner Verlag/Archiv/Picture-Alliance/DPA/AP Images, 5; Red Line Editorial/Chris Lemmens/ iStockphoto, 7; Andrew St. George/AP Images, 8, 28; Bettmann/Corbis/AP Images, 9, 10, 15, 16, 17, 24, 27, 29; AP Images, 11, 19, 21, 26; Miguel Vinas/Prensa Latina/AP Images, 13; Herman Hiller/World Telegram & Sun/Library of Congress, 14; Phil Stanziola/World Telegram & Sun/Library of Congress, 20; Department of Defense/AP Images, 22

**ISBN**
978-1-63235-127-2 (hardcover)
978-1-63235-170-8 (paperback)
978-1-62143-222-7 (hosted ebook)

**Library of Congress Control Number: 2015933982**

Printed in the United States of America
Mankato, MN
June, 2015

STORY
LIBRARY

Go beyond the book. Get free, up-to-date content on this topic at 12StoryLibrary.com.

# TABLE OF CONTENTS

# EUROPE IS DIVIDED AFTER WWII

During World War II (1939–1945), German Nazis took over many European countries. When Germany lost the war, the Nazis were pushed out of these countries. Nazi-controlled governments, schools, and businesses had to be rebuilt. Europe was divided into eastern and western sections. This division was called the "iron curtain." The United States, Great Britain, and Canada helped Western European countries rebuild. The Soviet Union aided Eastern European countries.

After World War II, much of Europe was left in ruins.

The iron curtain didn't just divide countries. It divided how people lived. Like the Soviets, the new governments in Eastern European countries were communist. In a communist government, the government owns everything. So in Eastern Europe, governments owned all the businesses and farms. They controlled schools and the news. The people living there had no freedom of speech. They could not own property.

Some people in Eastern Europe wanted the freedom of noncommunist countries.

## CHURCHILL NAMES CURTAIN

On March 5, 1946, Winston Churchill spoke at Westminster College in Fulton, Missouri. Churchill had been the prime minister of Great Britain. He talked about keeping people safe from war and unfair governments. He spoke about the right to live in freedom. He said an "iron curtain" had fallen across Europe. He was the first person to use this term to describe the situation there.

Communist governments fenced borders to keep people in. Soldiers manned guard towers on the borders. People who tried to cross into noncommunist countries illegally were oftentimes shot. But the iron curtain wasn't just a physical division. It symbolized the hostility between two ways of life.

## 4,225
Length, in miles (6,799 km), of the iron curtain.

- After World War II, Europe was split into western and eastern sections.
- Western Europe was aided by the United States, Great Britain, and Canada.
- The Soviet Union helped Eastern Europe rebuild.
- The iron curtain was the border between communist Eastern Europe and noncommunist Western Europe.

The Soviet Union supplied Berlin, Germany, with a shipment of butter, among other aid.

# WORLD WAGES COLD WAR

The effects of the iron curtain spread worldwide. The Soviet Union and the United States became fierce rivals. They competed to recruit other countries to their side. If a country appeared to be adopting a communist government, the Western powers issued a threat. If a country favored the West, the communists threatened it. The two sides spied on each other.

Neither side wanted a real war like World War II had been. Instead, they fought a war of words. Western leaders spoke out against the communists. They warned people about the communist threat. Communist leaders told people that the West was the enemy. This was called the Cold War, a struggle with no fighting.

Countries around the world took sides. In 1949, the western nations formed the North Atlantic Treaty Organization (NATO). An attack on one NATO country would bring the others into the fight. In 1955, the communist countries created the Warsaw Pact. An attack on one member in the Pact would be an attack on all. It also set up one military force under the Soviet Union. Tension built on both sides of the Cold War.

## 12
### Number of countries that founded NATO.

- The United States and the Soviet Union were rivals in the Cold War.
- In 1949, some noncommunist western nations formed the North Atlantic Treaty Organization (NATO).
- In 1955, communist countries created the Warsaw Pact.

NATO countries
Warsaw Pact Countries
Neutral Countries

Finland

Norway

Sweden

Denmark

Soviet Union

Netherlands

Great
Britain

Ireland

East
Germany

Poland

Belgium

West
Germany

Czechoslovakia

N

W        E

S

France

Switzerland

Austria

Hungary

ATLANTIC
OCEAN

Italy

Yugoslavia

Romania

Albania

Bulgaria

BLACK SEA

Portugal

Spain

Turkey

Greece

MEDITERRANEAN SEA

Europe during
the Cold War

# FIDEL CASTRO SEIZES POWER

After communism arose in Europe, it spread to other countries too. One of those countries was Cuba. Cuba is an island in the Caribbean, approximately 90 miles (145 km) from Florida. Fidel Castro would eventually bring communism to power in Cuba.

Castro was born on August 13, 1926. The son of a planter, he grew up wealthy. But he witnessed many Cubans in poverty. He wanted to help. In 1951, he ran for Cuba's House of Representatives. But General Fulgencio Batista overthrew the government. As Cuba's new leader, Batista canceled the election.

On July 26, 1953, Castro led 160 rebels in an uprising against Batista. They attacked Cuba's second largest military base. More than half of Castro's men were killed or captured.

Fidel Castro

## CUBA SERVES AS US PLAYGROUND

Before Castro took power, Americans often traveled to Cuba for vacation. At night, they went to clubs. They listened to jazz and danced. Airlines offered special flights to Cuba. Fancy hotels prospered. Many thought of this nation as an extension of the United States.

Castro read the oath of office to become prime minister of Cuba on February 16, 1959.

Castro spent two years in jail. When he was freed, he and his brother went to Mexico. They planned another rebellion.

On December 2, 1956, Castro returned to Cuba with 84 men. After losing 72 men, those remaining fled to the mountains. But as guerrillas, Castro's troops continued to attack.

Over the next few years, Castro's rebellion grew popular. In January 1959, Batista fled Cuba. At first, Jose Miro Cardona served as prime minister in the new Cuban government. Miro Cardona had been part of Castro's revolution. Castro was made military commander-in-chief. But in February 1959, Miro Cardona resigned, and Castro became prime minister.

## 32

Castro's age when he took control of Cuba.

- Castro was unhappy with Batista's government.
- Castro led a revolution to remove Batista from power.
- Castro became prime minister of Cuba in 1959.

## THINK ABOUT IT

The workers and people in poverty supported Castro. Who do you think supported Batista?

9

# KENNEDY BROTHERS COME TO DC

While Castro was coming into power in Cuba, brothers John F. Kennedy and Robert Kennedy were beginning their political careers in the United States. Like Castro, the Kennedy brothers grew up wealthy. John Fitzgerald Kennedy was born May 29, 1917. He was the second of nine children. Robert Kennedy was born November 20, 1925. He was the seventh child.

The two brothers joined the navy in World War II. John commanded a fast-moving patrol torpedo boat. One night, a Japanese destroyer struck the boat. John was hurt, but he helped an injured man to shore. In 1946, after the war, John was elected to the US Congress.

In 1951, Robert earned a law degree from the University of Virginia. After

John (left) and Robert Kennedy

he graduated, Robert managed John's 1953 Senate campaign. Robert also served on the Senate Subcommittee on Investigations. Senator Joseph McCarthy was in charge. This committee's goal was to identify communist spies secretly working in the US government. But McCarthy developed a reputation for harassing witnesses under interrogation. Bothered by these tactics, Kennedy resigned six months later. In February 1954, he rejoined the committee. He investigated how it worked. He wrote a report condemning what the committee had done.

In 1960, Robert managed John's presidential campaign. Once

# 43
## Age of John F. Kennedy at his inauguration.

- Brothers John and Robert Kennedy were both involved in US politics.
- John F. Kennedy became president in 1961.
- John appointed Robert as attorney general.

elected president, John appointed Robert attorney general. Robert enforced federal laws. He sought out corruption. The brothers worked for equal rights and to end poverty in the United States. They would both play important roles in the Cuban missile crisis.

John F. Kennedy became president in 1961.

# UNITED STATES FAILS AT BAY OF PIGS

The United States was not happy about Fidel Castro's new communist government in Cuba. Castro nationalized Cuban factories and farms. That meant that the government owned them. This hurt American companies in Cuba. Cuba also set up trade agreements with the Soviet Union. The two countries became allies.

In January 1960, President Dwight D. Eisenhower decided the United States needed to overthrow Castro. Cuba's alliance with the Soviets worried Eisenhower. The Central Intelligence Agency (CIA) recruited an invasion force to do the job. They selected Cuban men who had been forced into exile. The men would be trained for combat. Then, the United States would drop them into Cuba to overthrow the government there.

John F. Kennedy inherited this plan when he became president a year later. Kennedy wanted to take a stand against communism. He decided to go ahead with the plan. But he wanted it to look like Cuban rebels were leading the fight. That meant there couldn't be any US

## OPERATION MONGOOSE

Bay of Pigs was just one of the plans to change the government in Cuba. Operation Mongoose was a CIA plan to kill Castro to remove him from power. One idea was to poison his cigars. Another was to deliver poison capsules, hidden in makeup remover, to a female assassin. They also considered planting explosive seashells in the area he went swimming.

soldiers or obvious support from the United States.

In the early morning of April 17, 1961, 1,400 men landed at beaches along the Bay of Pigs on Cuba's southern shore. Their ships took heavy fire. Some ships got stuck on coral reefs. Many supplies never made it to shore.

The invaders were in trouble. The US military planned to send aircraft to bring them out of Cuba. This would require both bombers and fighter planes. This was too risky to trust to the new Cuban pilots. US flight instructors replaced their Cuban students and flew the planes. But due to confusion over time zones, the bombers arrived before the fighters. The bombers were heavily damaged and had to retreat.

# 100

Approximate number of Cubans in the invasion force killed in the Bay of Pigs.

- The United States worried about Cuba's alliance with the Soviet Union.
- Using exiled Cuban fighters, the United States planned an invasion to overthrow Castro.
- The invasion failed.

Most of the invaders were forced to surrender. Some were killed. People in Cuba realized that the United States was behind the invasion. The Bay of Pigs was a disaster.

Cuban soldiers inspect a plane shot down during the Bay of Pigs.

# KHRUSHCHEV CALLS FOR RESPECT

After the Bay of Pigs, Cuba began to rely more on its Soviet allies for military defense. Nikita Sergeyevich Khrushchev was the leader of the Soviet Union. Khrushchev wanted to protect communist countries and their allies from the West. He would become another major player in the Cuban missile crisis.

Khrushchev was born on April 15, 1894. His family lived in a small farming village. When he was a teenager, his family moved to Yuzovka, a mining town. Khrushchev went to work in the town's coal mines. Like many workers, he joined the Communist Party. In 1929, Khrushchev moved to the Soviet capital, Moscow. He became an important party member. He worked closely with Soviet leader, Joseph Stalin. Then Nazi Germany invaded Russia. Khrushchev aided those who fought the Nazis. After the

Khrushchev and Castro (center) make their way through a crowd.

war, Khrushchev coordinated the recovery. He worked to get farms, coal mines, and steel mills working again.

When Stalin died in March 1953, Khrushchev became the next party secretary to lead the Soviet Union. Khrushchev had seen too much poverty and destruction in the Soviet Union. He wanted to increase agriculture. He believed this would improve the people's lives.

For things to improve, Khrushchev knew his people had to be safe. He was willing to coexist with capitalist countries. But he wasn't sure that they were willing to do the same. The United States had coordinated the Bay of Pigs. Khrushchev worried that the United States would try to attack other communist countries. But he had a plan to increase Soviet power over the United States—and it involved Cuba.

## 15
### Age of Khrushchev when he went to work in the mines.

- Khrushchev became party secretary of the Soviet Union in 1953.
- Khrushchev and Castro built an alliance between their two countries.
- He worried that the United States would try to attack the Soviet Union and other communist countries.

Nikita Sergeyevich Khrushchev

# PLANE SPIES MISSILES IN CUBA

The United States knew that Cuba was now an ally of the Soviet Union. In spite of this, the US military was not worried about an attack from Cuba. They were more concerned about the politics of their communist neighbor. They were anxious about trade with Cuba. But they were not worried about a war.

All that changed on October 16, 1962. On that day, National Security Advisor McGeorge Bundy met with Kennedy. He showed the president photos from a U-2 high-altitude spy plane. The Air Force used these planes to secretly photograph what enemies of the United States were doing.

The photos had been taken two days earlier on October 14. They showed Soviet missile sites in Cuba. The sites were in the process of being built. Missiles were being assembled there. They were medium-range

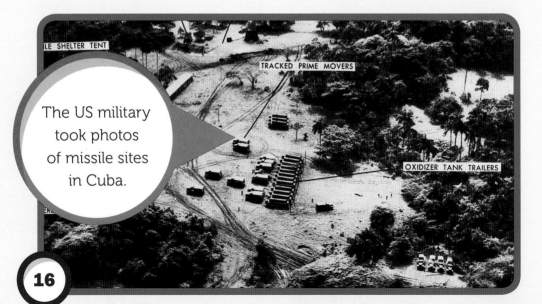

The US military took photos of missile sites in Cuba.

ballistic missiles. Such missiles could reach the United States. They could carry nuclear bombs.

A nuclear attack on the United States would be deadly. But the Soviets did not know that the United States knew about the weapons yet. Kennedy had to do something—fast.

# 40
Number of missile launchers the United States found in Cuba.

- On October 16, 1962, Kennedy was shown photos of Soviet medium-range missiles and launching sites in Cuba.
- Medium-range missiles in Cuba could reach the United States.
- The Soviet Union did not know that the United States had discovered the missiles.

The photos showed missiles and the materials needed to launch them.

ERECTOR ON LAUNCH PAD

OXIDIZER VEHICLES

PROB HYDROGEN PEROXIDE TANKS

SILE READY BLDGS

FUELING VEHICLES

ERECTOR ON LAUNCH PAD

MISSILE ON TRAILER

17

# EXCOMM AND KENNEDY CONSIDER THE OPTIONS

Kennedy couldn't ignore the missiles in Cuba. He had to make a tough decision. Kennedy met with his advisors, the Executive Committee of the National Security Council (EXCOMM). Robert Kennedy was on the committee too.

EXCOMM discussed several solutions to the problem. Each had strengths and weaknesses. Military advisors wanted to bomb the missiles. Their other recommendation was to invade Cuba. They wanted a fast solution so the Soviets couldn't strike back.

Politicians on the committee didn't want a war. They worried that Warsaw Pact–countries would come to Cuba's aid. The politicians wanted Kennedy to warn Castro and Khrushchev first. They wanted him

to tell the leaders that the missiles had to go or else the United States would attack.

Kennedy didn't like either approach. Instead, he decided to use the US Navy to blockade Cuba. That way no more Soviet missiles or supplies

## SECRETS RECORDED

From the first time EXCOMM met, Kennedy recorded the discussions. A microphone had been installed in the Cabinet Room's light fixture. Another was in his desk in the Oval Office. With these recordings, Kennedy made a permanent record of all discussions. The public didn't know about these tapes until 1973.

## THINK ABOUT IT

Every option EXCOMM discussed had risks. What decision would you have chosen? Why?

- Kennedy met with EXCOMM to decide what to do about the missiles in Cuba.
- Military advisors wanted to invade Cuba.
- Politicians wanted Kennedy to avoid war.
- Kennedy decided to blockade Cuba and insist that the missiles be removed.

would reach Cuba. He wouldn't lift the blockade until the missiles were out of the country. If the Soviets refused to remove the missiles, the United States would invade Cuba.

Kennedy had gone along with the CIA's plans for the Bay of Pigs. This time, he went against his advisors. He chose the blockade.

Kennedy discussed his plans with his brother Robert and other EXCOMM members.

# MISSILES CAPABLE OF DESTROYING US CITIES

On October 22, 1962, Kennedy appeared on television. He needed to address the American people about the threat of the missiles in Cuba. Usually, he chatted with reporters. But this night was different. It was time to tell the American people what was going on directly.

Kennedy spoke about the missiles in Cuba. He said they

Protesters urge Kennedy to be careful.

## POWERFUL MISSILES

The Soviets installed a variety of missiles in Cuba. Approximately 42 of the missiles were medium-range ballistic missiles. These missiles could travel 1,266 miles (2,037 km). Each missile was more than 60 times as powerful as the atomic bomb the United States dropped on Hiroshima, Japan.

could strike Washington, DC or the Panama Canal. They could strike Cape Canaveral, Florida, or Mexico City. Nowhere in the southeastern United States was safe. Every city in Central America and the Caribbean lay in danger.

Kennedy explained that he warned Cuba not to attack any American city. To Kennedy, this meant cities in Central America and South America too. If they did, he said the United States would attack the Soviet Union.

On television, Kennedy told the American people about his plan. The US Navy would surround Cuba. No ship carrying weapons would pass. People around the world waited to see what would happen.

Kennedy spoke about the crisis on national television.

## 17
Number of minutes that Kennedy's speech lasted.

- On October 22, 1962, Kennedy told the American people about the missiles in Cuba.
- Kennedy explained that the US Navy would stop any ships traveling to Cuba.

## THINK ABOUT IT

Imagine you are living during the Cuban missile crisis. How would you feel about Kennedy's plan?

# US NAVY QUARANTINES CUBA

Kennedy called his planned blockade of Cuba a *quarantine*. The US Navy surrounded Cuba. Ships approaching Cuba would be stopped. It didn't matter if the ship was Soviet. No weapons would reach Cuba. Khrushchev warned that if a Soviet ship was sunk, he would fight back.

US missiles were readied. Bombers carried nuclear weapons. US submarines with nuclear weapons lurked near the Soviet Union. The United States waited to see if they would need to use their weapons.

Several ships were allowed to pass through the blockade. An East German passenger ship sailed through. The navy only cared about ships carrying goods, not people. On October 25, a Soviet cargo ship approached. The tanker had no deck cargo. Tankers carry liquids, like fuel. The captain said he had no banned items. The ship was allowed to pass.

As the quarantine continued, Kennedy and Khrushchev

A Soviet ship on its way to Cuba

worked toward an agreement. Many members of EXCOMM still argued for war. But Kennedy believed a better solution was possible. He and Khrushchev just had to reach it.

Kennedy and his advisors were ready to order a strike if necessary.

## 42,000
### Number of Soviet troops in Cuba.

- Kennedy called his blockade of Cuba a quarantine.
- The quarantine kept more weapons from reaching Cuba.
- Kennedy negotiated with Khrushchev to try to reach a peaceful solution.

# CUBANS DOWN US PLANE

Khrushchev and Kennedy both wanted to avoid war. But limited communication made it difficult. There were no direct phone lines. They spoke different languages. This meant they had to work through their embassies and use translators.

Khrushchev wrote Kennedy letters. In one, he told Kennedy he would only pull out of Cuba if Kennedy promised not to invade it. Kennedy wanted to discuss this letter with EXCOMM. Then, another letter arrived. Khrushchev also wanted the US Jupiter missiles removed from

A photo of what was believed to be wreckage of the U-2 plane

# 15

Number of Jupiter missiles in Turkey at the time of the Cuban missile crisis.

- On October 27, a US plane was shot down over Cuba.
- Kennedy agreed that he would not invade Cuba if the Soviets removed their weapons there.
- Kennedy secretly agreed to remove missiles from Turkey.

## WHERE WAS CASTRO?

Castro knew that Khrushchev and Kennedy were negotiating. But he was not included. During the negotiations, Castro contacted Khrushchev. He told Khrushchev that the Cuban people were willing to sacrifice themselves. He said Khrushchev should strike first. Khrushchev was shocked that Castro pushed so hard for war.

Turkey. They were medium-range ballistic missiles. The United States had placed them there for defense. They thought the Soviets would be less likely to attack NATO countries for fear that the United States would launch these missiles.

Meanwhile, the USS *Oxford* floated off Cuba. The US ship was there to listen. It often heard radar systems being tested. On October 27, it heard radar lock on to a U-2 spy plane. In minutes, an US pilot had been shot down.

The first shot had been fired. This day would be called Black Saturday. Tensions rose. EXCOMM pushed

Kennedy to launch missiles. Soviet advisors pushed Khrushchev to attack. They didn't want Kennedy to have the chance to strike.

Kennedy sent his brother Robert to the Soviet embassy. On October 28, Robert had a message for the world. The United States agreed to not invade Cuba. But Robert also had a secret message from the president. The United States secretly agreed to remove the missiles from Turkey. But the Cuban missiles had to be removed first. On October 29, Khrushchev agreed to the terms.

# CRISIS SERVES AS A WARNING

Khrushchev removed the Cuban missiles. Kennedy removed the missiles from Turkey. But both powers knew the world had come far too close to nuclear war. They couldn't let it happen again.

The first step was better communications. Eight months after

> People in New York City protest nuclear weapon testing in the Soviet Union.

the crisis, a hotline was installed. This phone linked the Kremlin, the seat of the Soviet government, and the White House. As a backup, a teletypewriter linked Washington, DC to Moscow. This device printed written messages sent from a telephone call. Since 1971, the capitals have also been linked by satellite.

The leaders also saw that nuclear weapons were part of the problem. In 1963, they signed the Limited Test Ban Treaty, along with several other countries. No more nuclear tests could be made underwater. They could not take place in the air over the earth. Even tests in outer space were banned. Later treaties limited the creation of new nuclear weapons. After coming so close

# 13
## Number of days the crisis lasted.

- The Cuban missile crisis made world powers realize that nuclear war must be avoided.
- Bans on nuclear weapons testing and creation limited the threat of nuclear war.

to nuclear war, many nations were willing to limit their nuclear power if other countries did the same.

Khrushchev gives a speech at the 1963 signing of the Limited Test Ban Treaty.

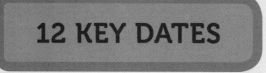

# 12 KEY DATES

**April 4, 1949**
The North Atlantic Treaty
Organization (NATO) is formed.

**May 14, 1955**
The Warsaw Pact is signed.

**February 16, 1959**
Fidel Castro becomes prime minister
of Cuba.

**April 17, 1961**
The Bay of Pigs invasion is a
disaster.

**October 14, 1962**
A U-2 plane photographs missiles
in Cuba.

**October 16, 1962**
Kennedy sees photos and calls
EXCOMM meeting.

**October 22, 1962**
Kennedy appears on television and
announces plan to quarantine Cuba.

**October 26, 1962**
Khrushchev sends first letter saying
he will the remove missiles if the
United States promises not to
invade.

**October 27, 1962**
Khrushchev sends second letter
saying he will the remove missiles if
the United Nations removes missiles
from Turkey. A U-2 plane is shot
down over Cuba.

## October 28, 1962

Kennedy proposes a solution. The United States will not invade. Soviets will remove missiles from Cuba. Secretly, the US missiles will be removed from Turkey.

## October 29, 1962

Khrushchev accepts Kennedy's terms.

## August 5, 1963

The Soviet Union, the United States, and several other countries sign the Limited Test Ban Treaty.

# GLOSSARY

**alliance**
A union between two or more countries that agree to help each other.

**blockade**
To use ships or soldiers to close a place off.

**capitalist**
To be part of a government system in which individual people own property.

**communism**
A system of government in which all property is owned by the government.

**exile**
To be forced to leave a country or city.

**guerrilla**
A fighter who uses sudden sneak attacks.

**interrogation**
The act of questioning someone.

**invasion**
When enemy military enters another country.

**negotiate**
To try to reach an agreement.

**quarantine**
To isolate or separate.

**tanker**
A ship that carries liquids.

**uprising**
An effort, usually involving violence, to change a government or leader.

# FOR MORE INFORMATION

## Books

Immell, Myra. *Perspectives on the Cuban Missile Crisis.* Detroit, MI: Greenhaven Press, 2011.

Jeffrey, Gary. *The Cuban Missile Crisis.* New York: Crabtree Publishing, 2014.

Samuels, Charlie. *The Cuban Missile Crisis.* New York: Gareth Stevens Publishing, 2014.

Senker, Cath. *Kennedy and the Cuban Missile Crisis.* Chicago: Heinemann, 2013.

## Websites

History.com: The Cold War
www.history.com/topics/cold-war

National Geographic Kids: Cuba
www.kids.nationalgeographic.com/explore/countries/cuba

Social Studies for Kids: The Cuban Missile Crisis
www.socialstudiesforkids.com/articles/ushistory/cubanmissilecrisis1.htm

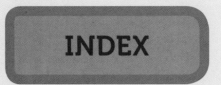

# INDEX

## About the Author

Sue Bradford Edwards writes nonfiction for children and teens, working from her home in St. Louis, Missouri. Her writing for young readers covers a wide range of topics, including science and history.

## READ MORE FROM 12-STORY LIBRARY

Every 12-Story Library book is available in many formats, including Amazon Kindle and Apple iBooks. For more information, visit your device's store or 12StoryLibrary.com.

# ABBY SUNDERLAND
## Alone on the Indian Ocean

BY XINA M. UHL

Published by The Child's World®
1980 Lookout Drive • Mankato, MN 56003-1705
800-599-READ • www.childsworld.com

Acknowledgments
The Child's World®: Mary Berendes, Publishing Director
Red Line Editorial: Design, editorial direction, and production
Photographs ©: Richard Hartog/AP Images, cover, 1, 8, 10; Shutterstock Images,
4; Stringer/France/Reuters/Corbis, 6; Wolfgang Kaehler/Corbis, 13; Oskari Porkka/
Shutterstock Images, 14; iStockphoto, 16; HO/Reuters/Corbis, 18; Red Line Editorial,
20; Bourchis-TAAF/SIPA/Newscom, 21

ISBN 9781634074704

LCCN 2015946303

Printed in the United States of America
Mankato, MN
December, 2015
PA02286

ABOUT THE AUTHOR
Xina M. Uhl loves history, travel, and pizza. She lives in southern California
with her family and a bunch of dogs.

# TABLE OF CONTENTS

# Chapter 1

# DEEP BLUE SEA

For days, the sea had been quiet. Wind gusted on and off, making the boat rock gently on the waves. The blue sky above and the blue water below were all that Abby Sunderland could see in every direction. A person could feel small with just a boat between herself, the endless ocean, and the lonely sky.

Not Abby, though. Even though she was just 16 years old, she had been sailing since early childhood. One of seven children, Abby was born into a family of sailors. In fact, the whole family had once lived aboard a boat for three years.

Abby knew what to do to keep her boat, *Wild Eyes*, in good shape. Check the lines that held down the sails. Listen for weather warnings on the radio. Add water to freeze-dried food for dinner. No one had to tell her to do these things. No one *could* tell her. Because Abby was alone on the boat.

With her father's help, Abby learned to pilot a boat when she was just 13. That was when she told her father that she wanted to sail around the world by herself someday. Abby's older brother Zac had the same dream. In 2009, 17-year-old Zac sailed a boat by himself around the world. He was the youngest person on record to do so. The record lasted only six weeks until a British teenager a few months younger than Zac broke it. By the time Abby turned 16, she and her family had decided to make Abby's journey happen. If she succeeded, she would be the youngest person ever to make such a trip.

By March 21, 2010, Abby had been sailing by herself for more than 50 days. As the day ended, the wind speed picked up. It measured about 25 to 30 **knots**, Abby figured. She yawned,

and lay down to sleep. Autopilot would steer the boat through the night.

At about 2:00 a.m., Abby jolted awake. She wondered, "Why are the dishes in my lap?" They belonged in the sink across the cabin. "And why am I sitting on the wall instead of on the bed?"[1] A large **swell** must have tossed the boat around. Alarms went off in her head.

The boat bounced upright again. Rushing above deck, Abby noticed that the autopilot had gone into standby, or sleep, mode. She fixed the course, and reset the autopilot. Then she checked the rest of the boat. The sails and the **mast** were fine. The radio was OK. Nothing had broken and there was no danger of sinking. Just a few things had been tossed around. She sighed in relief, and took a moment to calm down. It was the first time that Abby had felt scared. But it would not be the last.

◄ Abby was motivated by her older brother Zac for her attempt to sail around the world.

# Chapter 2

# PREPARING TO GO

Most people would not like being alone day after day, but Abby didn't mind it. On shore, other people made her nervous. She didn't talk much. But as the captain of her boat, Abby felt confident. The waves could be rough and the wind could be cold. Sometimes she had to steer, wet and tired, for hours. But Abby loved the challenge of sailing.

Sailing a boat around the world takes more than experience and passion, though. It takes a lot of money for a boat, supplies, equipment, repairs, and traveling to out-of-the-way ports. Abby's family couldn't afford to buy all that. When Zac took his trip, he looked for sponsors, or an organization that pays for a project.

Abby got a sponsor quickly for her trip: a store called Shoe City. With this money, she bought *Wild Eyes*, a 40-foot (12-m) sailboat. *Wild Eyes* was designed to travel across oceans.

On January 23, 2010, Abby set sail from her home in southern California. Her goal was to finish the **circumnavigation** without stopping. Abby had to get used to sleeping half of the time at night and half during the day. She started her trip by heading south, out of U.S. waters and into Mexican waters. Dolphins splashed around the **bow** and raced behind the boat. Other times they leapt high into the air.

Not long after she set sail, equipment problems cropped up. The autopilot needed more power. So did her phone and radio. Abby used solar panels and wind generators to make power. But they didn't make enough, and when it was cloudy, the solar panels didn't work. "I've hardly even started and I'm already heading in," Abby thought.[2]

**9**

# Chapter 3

# STRUGGLES AT SEA

Without equipment that worked, Abby could not continue her solo voyage. She was upset. She had wanted to make it through the entire trip without stopping. But Abby would have to take a break to repair the broken equipment.

On February 2, 2010, Abby landed in Cabo San Lucas, Mexico. There, she brought aboard more batteries and made repairs.

On February 6, 2010, Abby left Cabo San Lucas and started her journey again. Thirteen days later, she crossed the equator. There, it was hot and humid. The wind on which Abby depended to fill the sails and move the boat died down; she had hit the dreaded **doldrums**. The **current** threatened to move the boat the wrong direction.

Sometimes animals visited *Wild Eyes*. Squid even climbed aboard. So did flying fish. They jumped through the air and landed on the deck. A few birds flew overhead, despite being so far from land. Finally, the wind started blowing again, and the boat picked up speed.

Less than a week later, during the early morning hours, a terrible earthquake shook the coast of Chile. It was centered 22 miles (35 km) below the ocean's surface. On land, buildings collapsed. Electricity went out. On the sea, a tsunami, a large wave created by an earthquake, developed. Waves 50 feet (15 m) high struck the town of Constitución, Chile. Another wave about 8 feet (2.4 m) high traveled across the Pacific Ocean at almost 450 miles per hour (724 km/h). It slammed into the port of Talcahuano. Abby's mother called her on the satellite phone, worried that the tsunami would hit *Wild Eyes*.

Abby was almost 3,000 miles (4,828 km) offshore. Still, she didn't want to take any chances. Abby checked the boat, making sure that the sails and lines were in order. She closed the hatches. Then she waited, and waited some more. But nothing came, not even a big swell. Abby was safe for now.

## ABBY'S BLOG

While on her trip, Abby kept a blog to chronicle her experiences. People across the world following Abby's journey had lots of questions for her, such as:

*What are you taking with you for entertainment?* "I have a lot of fun books, my iPod, a couple of cameras, and I can always fish!"

*How did* Wild Eyes *get her name?* "When a great big wave breaks over the top of the boat and soaks you, most people recover with some pretty wild and crazy faces."

*What will you miss the most?* "My family for sure, especially my little sister. . . . I will miss people the most but it will be worth it. I will be doing something that I love and it will be a great adventure."[3]

▲ Cape Horn is considered the Mount Everest of sailing. It is also called "Sailors' Graveyard," due to the dangerous waves, currents, and icebergs.

Abby's next challenge was Cape Horn, at the southernmost tip of South America. Down there, between Chile and Antarctica, the weather was cold and windy, even in the summer. There, many ships had wrecked in the wild seas. Waves were huge—up to 100 feet (30 m) tall. The Southern Ocean at Cape Horn is one of the most dangerous areas in the world to sail. *Wild Eyes* would need to be in good working order now more than ever.

But one night before Abby reached the Cape, the autopilot stopped working. Luckily, she had a backup machine. Then the backup autopilot broke. Abby needed a working autopilot if she wanted to get around the Cape. Alone, cold, and wet, Abby knew it was going to be a long night before the autopilot could be fixed.

# Chapter 4

# OCEAN TO OCEAN

Cold and tossed about by choppy waves, Abby listened to the advice of two sailing experts over the boat's phone. The experts patiently talked her through repairing the autopilots. She worked through the night, taking parts from both devices. It was careful, frustrating work. Then, ten hours later, she flipped the switch of one autopilot. It worked! Abby was relieved. "I felt good about toughing it out. It really built my confidence," said Abby.[4]

On March 31, Abby became the youngest person to sail alone around Cape Horn. She was so tired from fixing the autopilot, though, that she slept right through the passage.

Now she was in the Atlantic Ocean, where it was warmer and sunnier. On some days, the wind was light, slowing her down. On other days it was foggy and rainy, and the wind blew harder.

Most of the time, all was quiet. But one stormy night Abby went above deck to adjust the sails. As she worked, a huge gust of wind struck the mainsail. As if a giant hand had smacked it, the boat tilted 80 degrees. Abby hung from the **boom** by the safety line. She managed to climb into the cockpit and adjust the **tiller**. The boat righted itself. She was safe once again.

At about the halfway point in her trip, Abby decided to head into port at Cape Town, South Africa. Even though she had fixed it earlier, the autopilot stopped working correctly again. Abby was disappointed. Though she had stopped in Cabo San Lucas before, she had planned on continuing the rest of her trip nonstop.

▲ The Port of Cape Town is located in Table Bay, South Africa, and is one of the busiest trade routes in the world.

The day that Abby headed into port marked more than 100 days of Abby sailing by herself. She stayed in Cape Town for more than two weeks, fixing equipment. On May 21, she set sail again, this time in the Indian Ocean.

During the second week in June, disaster struck. Storm after storm blew in. Gear spilled from the boat. The sails whipped back and forth, and tore. The autopilot started leaking, and the heater broke. Abby tried hard to remain calm. Huge waves knocked over *Wild Eyes* four times. The mast hit the water, but it didn't break. Abby hurried out of the cabin, steered the tiller, and righted the boat again.

She let out a sigh of relief. She was safe. But the storm kept on.

## JOURNEY ON KON-TIKI

Thirty-three-year-old Thor Heyerdahl also made a famous ocean voyage. But unlike Abby, he made his trip on a raft called Kon-Tiki. Thor wanted to prove wrong the experts who said ancient people from the Americas could not have sailed to Polynesia. He and five friends made Kon-Tiki from balsa logs in Peru. In 1947, over three months, they sailed 4,300 miles (6,920 km). They traveled all the way from South America to east of Tahiti. Despite this achievement, most of Heyerdahl's ideas about ancient sailing people have not been accepted by experts.

# Chapter 5

# ONE LONG WAVE

Abby was in the cabin of the boat, keeping out of the rain and wind. It was her 138th day at sea. Suddenly, a **rogue wave** struck, huge and strong. *Wild Eyes* rolled all the way over, turning Abby upside down. Fear clenched her stomach. Tools, a tea kettle, and silverware struck Abby. The roll continued. *Wild Eyes* righted itself again. Abby struggled out of the cabin. Despite the darkness, she saw the broken mast lying in the water. Lines were tangled everywhere. The boom had broken, too. Abby's heart sank. The boat could no longer sail. The trip was over.

Abby was drifting 2,000 miles (3,219 km) from land on a broken boat. Inside the cabin, she flipped on the emergency beacons to call for help. It might be weeks before anyone found her.

Numb and cold, Abby tried to be patient as she waited inside her wrecked boat. On June 12, 2010, a day after her boat became disabled, a French fishing vessel called *Ile de la Reunion* found Abby. The crew spotted the flare Abby had shot in the sky. Launching a small boat, they made their way to *Wild Eyes* and rescued Abby. Though she was cold and scared, she had only bumps and bruises.

News stations all over the world shared the good news that Abby was safe. But critics spoke out, too. They said Abby was too young to go on the trip and that her parents had risked her life. Abby's father defended the decision to let her go. "Sailing and life in general is dangerous. Teenagers drive cars. Does that mean teenagers shouldn't drive a car?" he said.[5]

MADAGASCAR

Indian Ocean

AUSTRALIA

CAPE TOWN

*Wild Eyes*

*Ile de la Reunion*

▲ This map shows where Abby's dramatic rescue took place.

Abby agreed with her father. She responded to critics by saying, "There are plenty of things people can think of to blame for my situation; my age, the time of year, and many more. The truth is, I was in a storm and you don't sail through the Indian Ocean without getting in at least one storm. Storms are part of the deal when you set out to sail around the world. As for my age, since when does age create gigantic waves and storms?"[6]

Abby did not make her goal of sailing around the world. But she did sail 12,000 miles. Now that she had survived a voyage that could have killed her, she was no longer shy and afraid of speaking up. Twelve hours after Abby returned to her home, her baby brother was born. Her parents named him Paul-Louis after the captain of the French fishing vessel that rescued her.

Abby knew that this wouldn't be her last adventure. She went off to college, learned to fly an airplane, and is considering sailing around the world again. One thing is certain: Abby Sunderland can make anything an adventure with her strength, courage, and determination.

▲ Abby's name was engraved on a plaque to celebrate her survival.

# GLOSSARY

**boom (boom):** A boom is a long pole used to stretch out the bottom of a sail. The location of the boom on the sail allowed Abby to shift the sails to catch the wind.

**bow (bou):** The bow is the forward area of a ship. Abby walked to the bow of the ship and looked over the edge into the ocean.

**circumnavigation (sur-KUHM-nav-i-gey-tion):** The act of circling the earth on a ship is known as circumnavigation. The first circumnavigation of the earth took place in 1522.

**current (KUR-uhnt):** A current is water moving in a certain direction. Abby's boat struggled against the strong current.

**doldrums (DOHL-druhmz):** The doldrums are a calm, quiet area in the ocean near the equator. *Wild Eyes* drifted, useless, in the doldrums for days before the winds picked up again.

**knots [nots]:** Knots are the nautical term for traveling one mile per hour on water. The wind moved *Wild Eyes* along at 25 knots.

**mast (mahst):** A mast is a long pole that extends upward from the bottom of a ship, which supports the sails and rigging. When the mast cracked in half, Abby knew that the ship could no longer sail.

**rogue wave (rohg weyv):** A rogue wave is a large, unexpected, and dangerous wave. For many years, scientists thought that rogue waves were myths.

**swell (swel):** A swell is a large wave. *Wild Eyes* bobbed up and down on the swell.

**tiller (TIL-er):** A tiller is a lever used to turn a boat's rudder from side to side. Abby adjusted the tiller and the boat headed to the left.

# SOURCE NOTES

1. Abby Sunderland. "Knock in the Night." *Abby's Blog*. Blogspot, 21 Mar. 2010. Web. 24 Jun. 2015.

2. Abby Sunderland. "One Week Out." *Abby's Blog*. Blogspot, 30 Jan. 2010. Web. 24 Jun. 2015.

3. Abby Sunderland. "Ask Abby!" *Abbysunderland.com*. n.p., n.d. Web. 5 Aug. 2015.

4. Abby Sunderland. Lynn Vincent. *Unsinkable: A Young Woman's Courageous Battle on the High Seas*. Nashville, TN: Thomas Nelson, 2011. Print. 102.

5. Aja Styles. "Teenager 'In Good Health' After Rescue Drama." *The Age*. Fairfax Media, 12 Jun. 2010. Web. 23 Jun. 2015.

6. Kelly Burgess. "And Now a Word from Abby Sunderland." *Los Angeles Times*. LA Times, 12 Jun. 2010. Web. 23 Jun. 2015.

# TO LEARN MORE

## Books

Johnson, Maureen. *Girl at Sea*. New York: HarperTeen, 2008.

Lundy, Derek. *The Way of a Ship: A Square-Rigger Voyage in the Last Days of Sail*. New York: Ecco, 2004.

Sunderland, Abby, and Lynn Vincent. *Unsinkable: A Young Woman's Courageous Battle on the High Seas*. Nashville, TN: Thomas Nelson, 2011.

## Web Sites

Visit our Web site for links about Abby Sunderland:
childsworld.com/links

*Note to Parents, Teachers, and Librarians: We routinely verify our Web links to make sure they are safe and active sites. So encourage your readers to check them out!*

# INDEX